STAGE 3

THRILLS AND CHILLS

**BY JONNY ZUCKER, PAUL STEWART
AND STEVE COLE**

**ILLUSTRATED BY DYLAN GIBSON,
JASON PICKERSGILL, LOIC BILLIAU,
PETE WILLIAMSON AND
DANIELA TERRAZZINI**

OXFORD
UNIVERSITY PRESS

CONTENTS

SUPERHERO STRUGGLE

BY JONNY ZUCKER
ILLUSTRATED BY DYLAN GIBSON

Setting the scene

Imagine visiting a theme park with amazing rides *and* its very own, real-life superheroes. It should be the best day out ever for Keisha and Jamal but there's a problem: instead of battling evil, the superheroes are fighting each other. Just think of the damage two superheroes could do …

Chapter 1

"What's going on?" asked Jamal, staring in astonishment at the wreckage of Montblue Theme Park.

The theme park sign lay smashed into pieces. Stalls had toppled over, spilling chips and ice-cream across the pavement. Posters had been ripped from the walls and the big wheel had ground to a halt. Crowds of bewildered, disappointed people were streaming towards the exit.

"I don't understand," said Keisha. "It was all supposed to be so special." She pulled out the newspaper article she and Jamal had read the day before.

NEW HOME FOR SUPERHEROES

Famous superheroes, Thunderclap and Light Shark, are alive and well in the heart of Montblue Theme Park.

The residents of Montblue town were perplexed when the superheroes seemed to disappear, three months ago. The pair had protected the town for many years, often arriving at crime scenes faster than the emergency services.

With no sightings of the heroes, people feared for their safety. "We're beginning to wonder if they've retired, been injured ... or worse," Detective Sergeant Marinder said just last week.

Then, yesterday, Montblue Theme Park made a surprise announcement: the superheroes have built themselves a home in the park.

"We're delighted to have Thunderclap and Light Shark here," said the park manager, Ray Owen. "As you know, the park has recently been closed for refurbishment. On Saturday we will re-open with a brand-new big wheel, roller-coaster and super-flume – and two *real* superheroes on site. People will have a chance to meet them face to face. This is a very exciting time for us and we can't wait to open on Saturday as Montblue *Superhero* Theme Park."

"It sounded so good. I wonder why it's all gone wrong," said Jamal. "If the superheroes are here, why aren't they doing anything to save the park?"

He'd been really looking forward to meeting Thunderclap and Light Shark. Although the superheroes had protected the town for years, people had rarely seen them close-up. They'd lived out in the mountains, only flying into the town when the need arose.

Feeling disheartened, Jamal turned towards the exit.

"Wait – let's not go yet," said Keisha.

7

At that moment, a tall man with a moustache and a badge saying 'Manager' pushed past. He was waving at the retreating crowds, calling, "Please don't go home! We can sort this out!"

"Can we help?" Keisha asked him.

The manager shrugged despondently, "I thought those two would be great for the park, but they're ruining it." He pointed to a tall green gate. "I've manged to get them to stay in there for now. I can't calm them down, though ..."

"Maybe we can," said Jamal.

Jamal and Keisha stepped through the gate and found themselves in a world transformed. The superheroes had built a tall glittering palace of silver and gold.

Unfortunately, at that moment, the superheroes were flying round the palace rooftop. They were in the middle of the most incredible fight, shouting and screaming at each other.

The children watched as sparks flashed from Light Shark's fingertips and exploded in a cascading blue shower close to Thunderclap's head.

With a deafening shout, Thunderclap flicked out his cloak and whipped it round Light Shark's waist, sending her somersaulting through the air.

Keisha and Jamal climbed a tower, drawing closer to the superheroes and listening to their argument.

"I had those Chase Street bank robbers in my grasp!" Thunderclap cried. "You let them go!"

"I got there before you!" Light Shark shouted back. "You were slower than a snail!"

"You should have left the diamond thieves to me!" yelled Thunderclap, flicking his cloak with such force that it sent the top of a turret crashing to the ground.

"Oh yeah? Then those crooks would have got away with the diamonds!" cried Light Shark, deftly dodging falling gold bricks.

The children paused on a balcony just below the superheroes.

"I don't believe it," gasped Jamal. "They're fighting so much they've nearly destroyed the park!"

"Maybe we can get them to stop," said Keisha. "Hello!" she called.

The superheroes paused, startled, but Light Shark had been about to shoot out a spark, and when she spun round towards Keisha, the spark flashed from her fingertips.

Quickly, Keisha leapt out of the way, but she lost her footing, slipped and tumbled off the balcony!

SUPERHERO
STRUGGLE

Chapter 2

Chapter 2

Jamal rushed to the edge of the balcony and peered over. Keisha was dangling from a window ledge, hanging by her fingertips.

Nervously, Jamal looked over his shoulder at the two superheroes. "*Do* something!" he pleaded.

Light Shark acted instantly. She dived from a turret and made a lunge for Keisha.

Unfortunately, Thunderclap dived at exactly the same time. He bumped into Light Shark just as she was about to reach Keisha – and managed to knock Jamal over the balcony on his way.

As Jamal fell, he reached for Keisha and miraculously grabbed her foot. So now there were two children dangling precariously from the window ledge.

"Look what you've done!" Light Shark shouted at Thunderclap. He was about to argue but realized that now was probably not the time. Two children were in terrible danger!

"We've got to work together," Thunderclap said. Light Shark nodded.

The two superheroes circled away from the wall and turned, ready to swoop towards the children.

However, at that moment, Keisha felt her grip slacken. Her fingers, already white with pain, were now completely numb and she couldn't hold on to the window ledge any longer. She let go.

Jamal and Keisha plunged towards the ground.

"Save us!" cried Jamal.

Thunderclap and Light Shark wasted no time. They stretched out their bodies into streamlined shapes and accelerated towards the children – just in time to sweep them into their arms before they hit the ground.

"Thanks for saving us," Keisha said breathlessly, "but it would have been better not to have caused the accident in the first place!"

"It was his fault," Light Shark began. "He's so clumsy, he got in the way!"

"You knocked her off the balcony with your spark first!" retorted Thunderclap.

"Please – STOP arguing!" said Keisha. "You should be ashamed of yourselves. You've almost destroyed the theme park – and you very nearly destroyed us!"

"We just don't understand," continued Jamal. "We used to be so proud of you. You saved our town so many times. People were seriously worried when you disappeared for months."

"Everyone was really excited when they heard you'd joined the theme park," said Keisha. "That's why this is all so disappointing."

The two superheroes looked at each other with red faces.

"What's going on?" asked Jamal.

Thunderclap shifted uncomfortably. "The thing is ... we're just not as good as we used to be."

"Once, we were incredible," said Light Shark wistfully. "Always first on the scene ..."

"Then we began to get a little tired," said Thunderclap. "Our powers weren't quite so sharp and we didn't always get to places on time. We tried to rest in our mountain home but we missed being superheroes."

"That's when we started arguing and blaming each other," said Light Shark. "Then we had a brilliant idea. We knew the theme park was being refurbished so we offered to become the resident superheroes."

"Well, that *was* a brilliant idea," said Jamal. "So what went wrong?"

"We're just not suited to it," said Light Shark sadly. "This morning, we were sitting in our chairs ready to meet and greet the public – but we got bored."

"Then the manager said the big wheel wasn't working," said Thunderclap.

"Yes – that bit wasn't our fault, it was a mechanical failure," said Light Shark. "We tried to get it working again, but we couldn't and we got frustrated."

"So you started fighting and nearly destroyed the park!" said Keisha.

Light Shark nodded guiltily.

"We can't just sit still and talk to people all day," said Thunderclap. "We're too fidgety. We might not be the best superheroes anymore, but we still need action!"

Jamal had been listening intently, frowning. Now his face cleared and he smiled at the superheroes.

"I know how you can have action!" he said. "You could show off your skills. How about putting on a daily stunt show?"

"Yes, and the big wheel doesn't need to work mechanically – you two could pull it round as you fly. Imagine: *The only wheel in the world powered by superheroes* – people would love it!" said Keisha.

By now Jamal and Keisha were thoroughly enjoying themselves – and the superheroes were, too.

"These are brilliant ideas," said Light Shark. "Let's go and tell the manager."

Thunderclap smiled at the children. "I think you've just saved the park – and us, too!"

Stunt Artists

BY JONNY ZUCKER

ILLUSTRATED BY JASON PICKERSGILL

Setting the scene

When you think of an artist, you probably think of a person who creates pictures and images. In fact, an artist can be anyone who is highly skilled at what they do. When a stunt is performed in a film, it makes you think that the character is doing something dangerous, but it is actually the stunt artist who is doing something dangerous – which they have been specially trained to do.

Stunt Artists

Whenever you see a film containing fight or action scenes, you can be sure that stunt artists are involved. For scenes that require dangerous moves, such as kicks, car chases or jumping off buildings, it's likely that the film's 'stars' are not performing those moves themselves. Instead, stunt artists perform the dangerous parts, and keep the actors out of harm's way.

Planning and training

Stunt artists are highly trained, plan carefully and use many safety devices to avoid getting hurt.

Mock fights

A fight that lasts seconds on screen can take hours of planning. Stunt co-ordinators are hired by a film, TV or theatre company to plan stunts and give instructions to artists. They plan each move carefully, and stunts are practised in slow motion several times. Stunt artists try not to hit or kick each other – each move is carefully designed to miss by a few centimetres.

▼ Sometimes actors do the fights themselves, as in *The Karate Kid*.

Jumps and falls

Jumping on to moving vehicles or falling from heights are regular features of a stunt artist's job. Usually there are safety nets or deep airbags set out below the jump, and sometimes the stunt artist wears a harness.

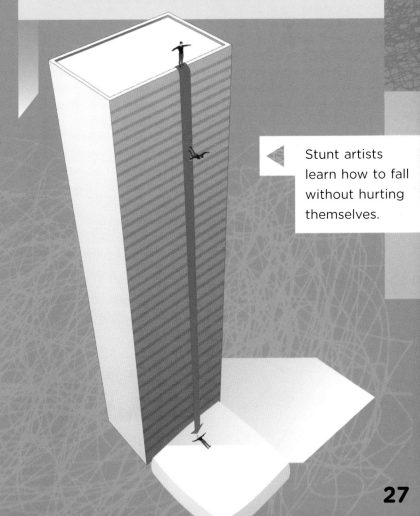

Stunt artists learn how to fall without hurting themselves.

Fire!

Scenes that involve fire are some of the most dangerous in film, especially when the scene shows a person catching fire.

The stunt artist wears a tight-fitting suit of fire-resistant material. This usually has gloves and a hood so that the hands and head are covered. Next, the artist is covered all over in a flammable gel. The costume is then covered in an outer material that burns easily, so the scene can be shot as quickly as possible. Paramedics and people with fire blankets and fire extinguishers must be at the scene.

▲ A fire stunt from *The World Is Not Enough*

Classic stunts

Here are two of the most famous stunts in the history of film.

Stagecoach (1939)

Yakima Canutt, one of the best stunt artists of his time, leaps on to horses that are pulling a wagon.

Safety Last (1923)

The image of the comedian Harold Lloyd
dangling from the hands of a clock is famous
all over the world. Before filming, the film crew
built the wall with the clock on top of the roof
of a building. This meant that if Harold fell,
he would land on mattresses laid on the roof,
rather than on the street far below.

Behind the wheel

Stunt driving is an extremely specialized skill. Cars used in stunt scenes have safety equipment, such as a roll cage and on-board fire extinguishers.

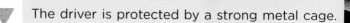

The driver is protected by a strong metal cage.

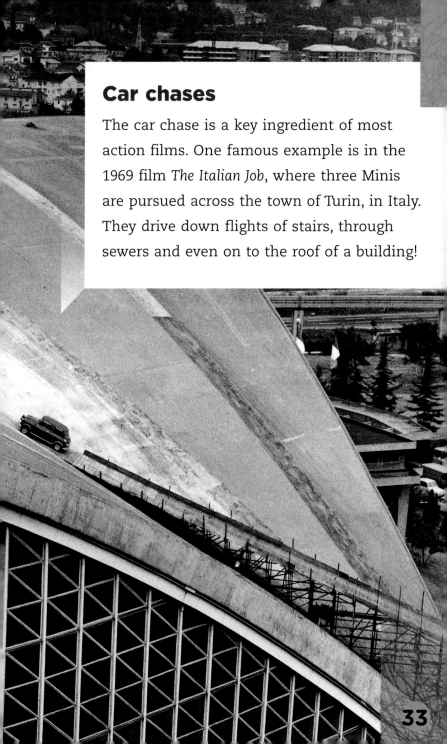

Car chases

The car chase is a key ingredient of most action films. One famous example is in the 1969 film *The Italian Job*, where three Minis are pursued across the town of Turin, in Italy. They drive down flights of stairs, through sewers and even on to the roof of a building!

What about technology?

You might wonder why any stunts are filmed 'live', when filmmakers can now create special effects using technology such as **CGI** or **'green screen'**. The answer is that many films use a mix of green screen, CGI, models, special effects and stunts.

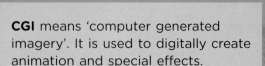

CGI means 'computer generated imagery'. It is used to digitally create animation and special effects.

Green screen is when a filmmaker takes shots of actors against a single-colour screen. The filmmaker can then superimpose the actors on to another scene.

Should stunts be replaced by CGI?

While stunt artists are extremely careful, the fact remains that stunts can be dangerous. There have been accidents. Stunt artists often get badly bruised, and sometimes even break bones while working on a film.

Given the hazards, some people have suggested that all stunts should be replaced by CGI. They worry that film directors take too many risks while trying to create the perfect action sequence.

However, other people argue that stunts are important for several reasons: audiences don't want to see only CGI sequences; stunt artists are willing to do the stunts and, furthermore, if films only use CGI, stunt artists will have no work!

In conclusion, perhaps stunts can remain part of action films, provided that directors always ensure the stunt artist is as safe as possible.

MY FRIEND ANDY

BY PAUL STEWART
ILLUSTRATED BY LOIC BILLIAU

Setting the scene

This story looks ahead to a possible future. You will recognize the setting: a skateboard park where the local kids meet up. However, you might be surprised by a futuristic twist that is revealed as the story unfolds ...

Chapter 1

Andy was the new boy. He joined our class in the middle of term. Short and thin, with dark brown hair and eyes, he was always friendly and helpful. I liked him. Most of the class did. For me, though, the best thing about him was that he loved skateboarding.

My name's Logan, by the way. I got my *first* skateboard when I was seven, then a new one every birthday since. There's a skateboard park near my house with a wide concrete bowl, plus some half-pipes and a couple of ramps. I used to go there every weekend to practise on my own. Now I go with Andy.

I'm not bad at skateboarding, but Andy ... he's amazing. When he's on his board, it's as though he's got wings.

That's probably why Ty, Mozza and Dek didn't much like him. They're rubbish at skateboarding. Ty's always falling off. Mozza recently broke her ankle when a 360 flip went wrong. And Dek ... don't get me started.

One Saturday, Andy and I went to the park to find Dek, Ty and Mozza already there. Dek was down on the flat concrete, trying – and failing – to do an ollie.

It's pretty basic, an ollie. It's when you and the board leap into the air. You have to jump up and kick down on the back of your board at the same time. Timing is everything.

Unfortunately, timing wasn't Dek's strong point. He just couldn't get the board off the ground. So Andy, being helpful and friendly and that, stopped skateboarding to teach Dek how to do it.

"Crouch lower," he told him. "Bend your knees more, and shift your front foot closer to the middle of the board. That's it. Make sure you pull your knees up to your chest when you jump."

Dek kept trying, and every jump he did was a bit higher than the one before. Soon he was actually looking pretty good.

"That's it," said Andy. "Just be careful when you come down. If you've got both feet in the middle of the board, then ..."

There was a loud clunk, followed by a splintering *crack*, followed by a howl of rage.

"... you'll break it," said Andy quietly.

Dek's face darkened. "That skateboard wasn't cheap," he shouted, "and now it's broken." He turned on Andy. "Because of you!"

"Yeah," said Ty and Mozza, egging him on.

Andy backed away. Dek took a step towards him, with Ty and Mozza close behind.

"So, what are you gonna do about it?" Dek demanded. "Eh?" He shoved Andy hard in the chest.

Andy staggered backwards and fell to the ground. Dek stood over him, his fists clenched.

"Get up!" he shouted.

Andy didn't get up. I don't blame him. Dek's twice his size, and I wouldn't have been much help either. Not if Ty and Mozza joined in. Suddenly angrier than I've ever seen him, Dek picked up a piece of his broken skateboard and hurled it at the ground. A massive splinter broke off and hit Andy in the arm. The jagged wood cut through the sleeve of his shirt and buried itself in his skin.

For a moment, Dek stared in horror. Then, realizing what he'd done, he spun round and the three of them ran off. I turned to Andy. I couldn't believe he wasn't crying out with pain.

"Let me look at that arm," I said.

"No, it's fine," he said, twisting sharply away – and that's when I saw it.

The skin had been badly torn, but there was no blood or bone beneath it. Instead, my gaze fell upon what looked like the inside of a machine: metal plates, screws, wires, and a long steel rod that had been bent in two.

MY FRIEND ANDY
Chapter 2

Chapter 2

I didn't know what to think. Or say. I just stood there staring down at him as Andy pulled the piece of broken skateboard from his arm and tossed it away. Then he tried to stand up, but found he couldn't.

"My ALU's malfunctioned," he said. I must have looked puzzled, because he added, "Arms and Legs Unit. Can you get me home, Logan?"

I'd never been to Andy's house before, and as I helped him walk, he gave me directions. Apart from that, we didn't talk. I couldn't stop thinking about what I'd just seen.

My new friend Andy was some kind of robot.

But how? It made no sense. Of course he was human, and yet ...

"It's that one," he said, breaking into my thoughts, and I looked up to see a grand mansion ahead of us.

As we walked up the long gravel driveway, we passed gardeners mowing the lawns and tending the flower beds. A butler met us at the front door. He looked Andy up and down. Then, without saying a word, he took us inside the house, where an army of servants was busy cleaning. He stopped at a door and knocked.

"Enter," came a voice, and Andy and I went inside.

An old man was sitting at a desk. With his messy white hair and steel-rimmed glasses he looked like an eccentric professor. When he saw us, he jumped up and hurried across the room to inspect Andy's arm.

"What happened?" he asked.

Andy remained silent, so I answered for him. "He got into a fight with a boy at the skateboard park," I said, and went on to tell him everything.

"You're Andy's friend, are you?" he asked.

"I'm Logan," I said. I looked at Andy. "And you ... he ..."

"I'm Doctor Gabinelli," said the man. "I made Andy, like I made all the robots here." He smiled. "But Andy is my masterpiece. That was why I sent him to school. I wanted to know whether anyone would notice that he wasn't human. Did *you* notice, Logan?"

"Well," I said. "Looking back, there were a couple of things. He's brilliant at IT and Science, but hopeless at poetry. I've never seen him eating, and he never gets my jokes ..."

"Yes, I've been working on his sense of humour," said Doctor Gabinelli. "Anything else?"

I shrugged. "Maybe you should have made him a bit bigger and stronger," I said, "so that he wouldn't get picked on."

"Oh, Andy here is as strong as a bear," came the surprising reply. "But he's been programmed always to be friendly and helpful." Doctor Gabinelli sighed. "Now, because of that, it's going to take me weeks to repair him." He reached out and shook my hand. "Thank you, Logan, for bringing him home."

I realized it was time for me to go.

Andy was off school for five weeks in all. When he finally came back, he looked different – a little bigger, perhaps – though he was just as friendly and helpful as before.

Dek and a few others went up to him in the playground during morning break. I hung back, nervous about what was going to happen.

I needn't have worried though.

"I'm really sorry about your arm, mate," said Dek. "I shouldn't have got angry like that. How is it?"

"Fine, thanks," said Andy.

Dek nodded. "I got a new skateboard," he said. "The two of us should go up the park soon. You can teach me some tricks."

"That would be fun," said Andy.

Dek smiled. "By the way," he said. "I've been meaning to ask you. What's Andy short for? Andrew? Andreas ...?"

"Android," said Andy, and the others laughed.

They thought he was joking, but I knew better. Doctor Gabinelli might have upgraded Andy to be a bit bigger and stronger, but he still hadn't managed to give him a sense of humour. Andy was simply telling the truth.

THE BIONIC HUMAN IS COMING!

BY PAUL STEWART

Setting the scene

This text will tell you about ways that machines can be used as part of the human body, making use of computers, electronics and robotics. As you find out about the facts, you will also learn that there are lots of questions about what scientists should or should not do in the future. Reading the information will help *you* make decisions about these questions.

THE BIONIC HUMAN IS COMING!

The idea of the 'bionic human' – a person that is part human and part mechanical – has often been explored in science fiction, but how close is it to reality?

Huge advances in medicine and technology mean that mechanical body parts can now replace missing or damaged human body parts. Could scientists really create a fully operational bionic human being?

The history of replacing body parts

Prosthetics

For centuries, people have used **artificial** body parts, called prosthetics, to replace missing or damaged body parts. Some prosthetics, like artificial legs and false teeth, have a practical purpose – they enable people to walk and eat again. Others, like glass or acrylic eyes, are **cosmetic**, rather than functional.

This iron prosthetic arm was made in Spain in the 1500s.

Pacemakers like this are attached to faulty hearts to help them beat more regularly.

Transplants

During the 20th Century, it became possible to **transplant** human **organs** from one person to another, so a person who suffered kidney failure could receive a healthy kidney from someone else. In addition, machines, such as pacemakers could now be attached to organs to make them work better.

The science of bionics

In the 21st Century, prosthetics and transplants came together in the science of bionics: man-made mechanical systems that work just like parts of the human body. Today, bionics has made it possible to replace almost any human body part.

A modern bionic leg

The man with the bionic hand

Bertolt Meyer was born with a left arm that stopped at the elbow. In 2013, he was fitted with a mechanical hand. This bionic hand, with fingers powered by their own motors, is connected by **electrodes** to the muscles in Meyer's arm. Using his muscles, as well as an app on his phone, Meyer can open and close the artificial hand and rotate the wrist.

Bertolt Meyer using his bionic hand

Other bionic developments

Scientists have also produced mechanical versions of other human organs, including the kidneys, lungs and heart. This is useful because it could end the shortage of **organ donors**, so people don't have to wait so long for transplant operations.

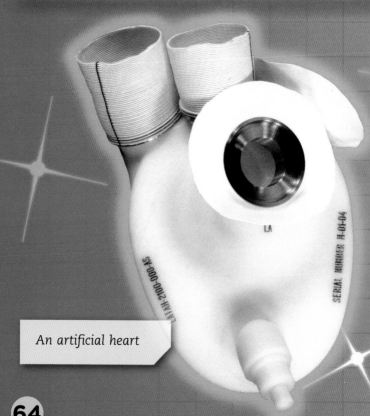

An artificial heart

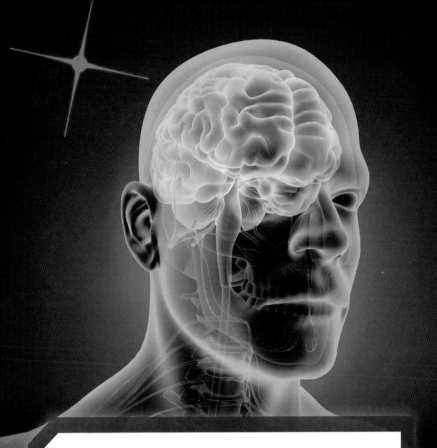

Nano memory cells – tiny artificial units that work like brain cells – are being developed. Scientists hope to use these to build an artificial copy of a brain.

In addition, scientists are carrying out experiments to connect the human brain to a computer, so that people can control any bionic unit they have been fitted with.

Making bionic body parts

Plastic, metal and electrical circuits, as well as 3D printing, are now being used to make bionic body parts to transplant into a living person. The next challenge for scientists is to build a completely artificial 'human' being.

A bionic human?

A model of an artificial 'human' that can walk, talk, hear and see – and has a beating heart – has already been made. It has robotic limbs, artificial organs and a system that pumps blood around the body, as well as a silicone face. At the moment, more than fifty per cent of the human body can be created in this way. However, the aim is to produce a one hundred per cent artificial bionic human.

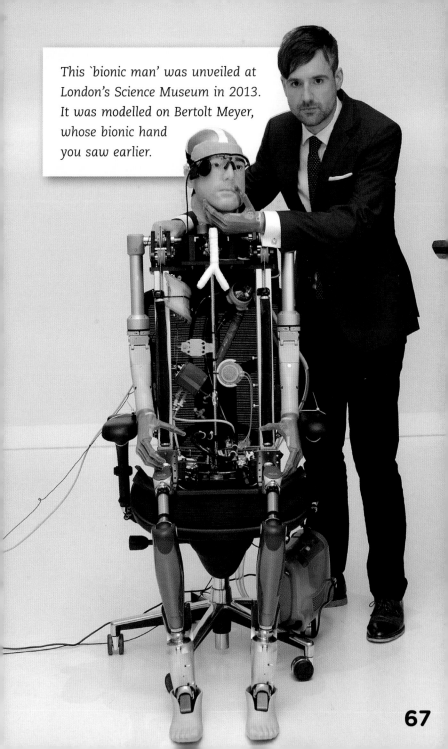

This 'bionic man' was unveiled at London's Science Museum in 2013. It was modelled on Bertolt Meyer, whose bionic hand you saw earlier.

67

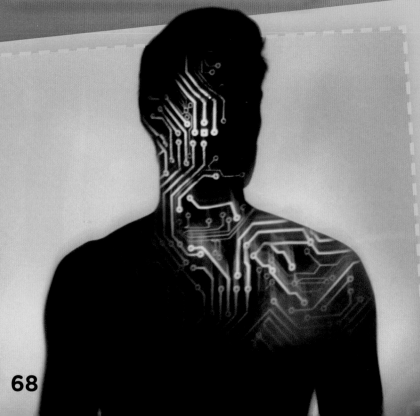

Moral questions

Advances in bionic technology raise some important questions, which we would be foolish to ignore.

- Firstly, how far can a human being still be considered human, if many of its body parts have been replaced?

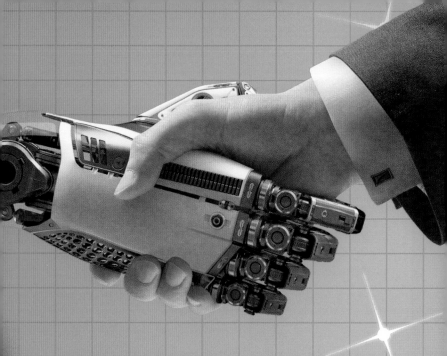

- Secondly, how advanced should the bionics be? A woman with a bionic arm is clearly still human. However, if her bionic eyes cannot only see everything humans can see, but are also infra-red and ultra-violet; or if her brain has the power of an advanced computer, then is she really 'human' at all?
- Thirdly, and most importantly, is it sensible to create bionic 'super-humans' that might one day replace us? It's a chilling thought!

Glossary

artificial something created by people rather than by nature

cosmetic for appearance only

electrode something which takes and passes on an electrical message

nano something on a really tiny scale

organ a working part of the body with a specific purpose

organ donor a person who gives one of their organs to someone who needs it

transplant to move something somewhere else

THE INVISIBLE THING

BY STEVE COLE
ILLUSTRATED BY PETE WILLAMSON

Setting the scene

It is late in the evening. Dad and the two children, Ewa and Artur, are sitting in their broken-down car in the middle of a fierce storm. Behind them looms a mysterious old house with creepy towers. Would you venture in?

It was a coal-black night, with a storm blowing so hard that the moon and stars had fled. In the back seat of Dad's car, Artur looked nervously at his sister Ewa. The car had broken down, and no one had any signal on their mobile phone.

"Great," said Ewa. "You realize, there's nothing around for miles!"

A flash of lightning showed she was wrong. Lit up at the side of the road was a sinister-looking house, with more towers and turrets than you could count. Lights glowed at the windows.

"That's a relief!" said Dad. "We can ask the people who live there for help."

Artur and Ewa got out of the car and hurried to the front porch. Dad was about to ring the doorbell, when the door creaked open.

A woman with wild, red hair and a long white coat came out. She had wide, staring eyes and a smile that was crammed with sharp white teeth. "Greetings!" said the woman. "I'm Doctor Theresa Punchbrush."

Artur and Ewa swapped a worried look, and followed their dad into a grand hallway stuffed with musty, old-fashioned furniture. The floorboards creaked and groaned under their feet.

"Our car's broken down, Doctor Punchbrush," said Dad. "May we use your phone to call a mechanic?"

"I haven't got a phone," said Doctor Punchbrush. "People kept calling me while I was working, so I dismantled it and rebuilt it as a toaster!" She smiled. "However, my assistant Marlon is a master-mechanic. He just *loves* fixing broken-down vehicles. But he's not all that easy to find. Let's see if he's lurking in my laboratory."

All three began to follow Doctor Punchbrush, but she shook her head. "Just your father," she told the children. "I don't want you to disturb my experiments. Wait here, please."

"Never mind, kids." Dad winked. "You won't have so far to run back to the car if anything spooky happens!"

Ewa rolled her eyes. "You're so not funny, Dad."

Doctor Punchbrush waved to them cheerily as she led Dad through a door in the wall.

As the door closed, Ewa and Artur heard a sinister noise through the sound of the storm, like a low, choking growl.

"What was that?" hissed Ewa.

The noise came again, a squealing roar followed by a strange snake-like rattling sound.

Artur began to shiver.

Suddenly, the front door burst open – but nobody was there!

"Come ..." came a low, rasping voice. "Come with meeeeeee ..."

"EEEEEK!" Artur and Ewa clung together, frozen in horror. The voice came closer, and they turned and fled up the staircase.

"COME ..." the voice rasped, as heavy footsteps came pounding up the stairs after them.

"It's following us!" Fear squeezed at Artur's heart. "What can we do?"

"Keep running!" Ewa cried. She could feel hot, sticky breath on the back of her neck. The invisible *thing* was right behind her. Its growling voice filled her ears.

"COME ... WITH ... ME ...!"

"No!" Ewa charged across the landing and back down the second staircase. "Leave us alone!"

Artur and Ewa were about to race outside, when Dad and Doctor Punchbrush returned.

"Ah," said Doctor Punchbrush. "*There* you are, Marlon!"

Artur frowned and indicated the thin air in front of him. "You mean this creepy creature is *Marlon*?"

"Sorry, children," said Doctor Punchbrush. "I told you Marlon would be difficult to find ... because he's *invisible*."

Dad's jaw dropped so far it nearly hit the floor. "You're working on *invisibility*, Doctor Punchbrush?"

"That's amazing!" Artur gasped. "But why was Marlon trying to scare us?"

"Wanted you ... to come ... with me ..." Marlon hissed again. "... to seeeeee your car. I just fixed it!"

"Ha!" laughed Doctor Punchbrush. "I told you he'd be eager!"

Ewa turned to Artur, red-faced. "That noise we heard outside was the car being fixed!"

Artur smiled, sheepishly. "I guess we should've played things cooler, but it's not every day you get chased by an invisible man!"

"Let's not make a habit of it," said Ewa.

"We'd better be going." Dad beamed. "Thank you for fixing it, Marlon!"

"There'll be no charge," Doctor Punchbrush assured him. "Now, farewell! Good luck! *Au revoir*!"

Dad, Artur and Ewa ran gratefully back through the rain to their car.

Dr Punchbrush watched them go. "Thanks for repairing their engine, Marlon, so we could send them on their way. Our invisibility project is far too important to be disturbed ..."

As she spoke, she faded from sight, and she and Marlon went on with their work.

BY STEVE COLE

Setting the scene

Some things are invisible because they are too small for our eyes to see. This information text is about living things – organisms – that are found all over the place: in your house, on your food and even in your own body! Some do useful jobs and others attack like an invading army, but they are all invisible without special equipment to see them.

INVISIBLE INVADERS

Micro-organisms – or microbes – are tiny living creatures that cannot be seen with the naked eye. You could fit several hundred on a single full stop.

Hi! Hello!
Hi there!
Hello! Hi!

No matter how clean you are, or however much you wash, there's no getting rid of these tiny, near-invisible **critters**. In fact, if you *did* get rid of them, you'd be a lot worse off, because microbes are often good for you … even if the thought of them might seem TOTALLY GROSS!

How many microbes are there?

There are more microbes on the planet than any other form of life – trillions and trillions and trillions of them. Some help us to live, others make us ill, but there's one thing they all have in common: they're super-good at hide and seek!

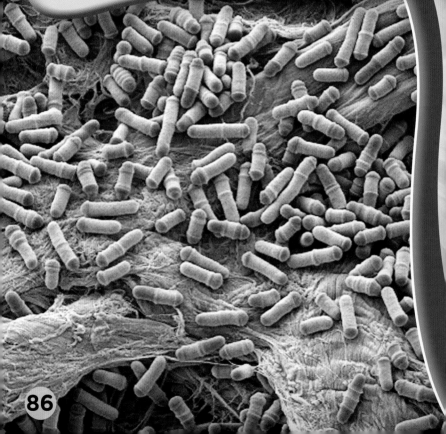

THERE ARE FIVE KINDS OF LIVING MICRO-ORGANISMS:

Bacteria

Under powerful microscopes, bacteria can look like rods, spheres or spirals. Different bacteria can affect our health in different ways, but since pretty much everything around us is smothered in them, they're hard to avoid!

DID YOU KNOW?

There are ten times more bacterial cells in your body than human cells! But don't panic – our bodies *need* these microscopic bugs. Without bacteria breaking down our food into **vitamins** and **minerals**, we'd be in big trouble.

Viruses

These tiny parasites can only survive inside the cells of other living things – such as us. They cause infectious diseases, like chicken pox or mumps.

Fungi

Some of these, like mushrooms, are very visible. But fungi can also be microbes, like mould, or even yeast (which helps make bread).

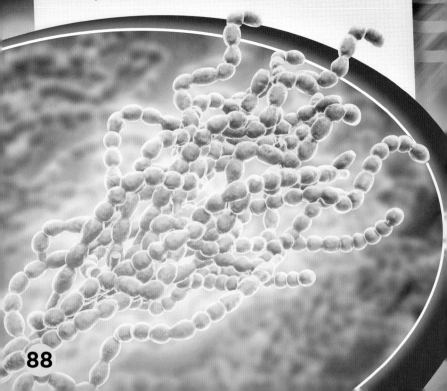

Algae

Algae are plant-like organisms that usually float in water. Seaweed is a large type of algae, but other algae are so minuscule, they can only be viewed using a microscope. Some algae are even used in toothpaste to stop it going too runny!

Protozoa

These single-celled organisms feed on bacteria and fungi, so they help **sewage** decompose. However, they're less helpful when they're causing horrible diseases like malaria and dysentery!

DID YOU KNOW?
When protozoa feed on sewage, they turn harmful substances into useful ones, like nitrogen.

They 'mite' be everywhere

Some tiny animals may never be seen, but they 'mite' be closer than you think. For instance …

Demodex spiders

Minuscule, eight-legged 'eyelash mites' live on your face in hair follicles (the tiny holes your hairs grow out of). They hang out in your eyebrows, eyelashes and all over your face, but stay calm – they actually do a pretty good job! They feed on dead skin cells and oils that build up there, and keep your skin healthy.

House dust mites

Found in almost every home, there may be *millions* of these tiny bugs living in your bedding, on your couch, or in your carpet. You'll never know, because they're invisible to the naked eye. Although they give some people allergies or sneezes, they're pretty much harmless for most of us.

The good, the bad and the algae

Just like human beings, there are good forms of microscopic organisms, and bad ones ...

WANTED

LIVE YOGURTS

FOR HEALTHY STOMACHS

As well as tasting good, these special yogurts contain 'good' bacteria that make our stomachs happier! Other foods good for your tum are miso soup and sauerkraut, which is made from fermented cabbage – YUM!

WANTED

RHIZOBIA

FOR HEALTHY SOIL

Soil needs nitrogen in order to grow
healthy crops, and rhizobia bacteria
can keep nitrogen in the soil by
infecting the plants' roots. We'd be
a lot hungrier without them!

NOT WANTED

SALMONELLA

MESSES UP YOUR GUTS

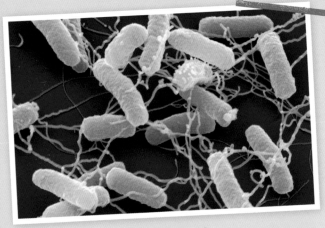

Despite its name, salmonella has nothing to do with fish! These bacteria cause food poisoning, which can give you sickness, fever, stomach cramps and diarrhoea! Salmonella is normally caught from contaminated chicken and eggs but there are many other sources, so always wash your hands before eating or preparing food!

NOT WANTED

TOO MUCH ALGAE

We need algae in our oceans, because they make oxygen, which helps keep fish (and us!) alive. However, too much algae use up more oxygen than they produce, so the fish and other underwater creatures die.

Glossary

cells   the smallest building
                    block of life (humans have
                    millions of cells, while some
                    creatures only have one cell)

critter   an animal

nitrogen   an important gas in the air

organism   anything that is alive,

oxygen   a gas in air and water
                    which keeps us alive

sewage   waste water and other
                    materials that travel
                    through sewers

vitamin/mineral a substance which helps
                    keep our bodies healthy

THE MIRACLE BEAST

BY STEVE COLE
ILLUSTRATED BY DANIELA TERRAZZINI

Setting the scene

Poets create pictures using words that can help you imagine something you have never seen. In this poem you will discover a creature that seems invisible – not because it is microscopic, not because it can actually disappear, but because it has to stay hidden away from people.

THE MIRACLE BEAST

"Now, all the creatures in the world,
That run and fly and swim and slide
Are in our books," the wise men say,
But *maybe* ... all the wise men lied.

Not everything that ever lived
Has found its way to printed fame,
Some creatures roam the earth and still
Have never once been given names.

Now, since your eyes cannot behold
The awesome wonder of my kind,
I'll paint a picture that will bring
My image to your youthful mind:

I stand quite tall, eight feet or more,
My skin is tough and thick with hair,
My ears are pointed like my horns,
I think I'd give you quite a scare!

As sharp as blades, my pointed fangs
Could rip the flesh and pierce the heart,
And break the bones and pop the eyes,
And tear my hapless prey apart ...

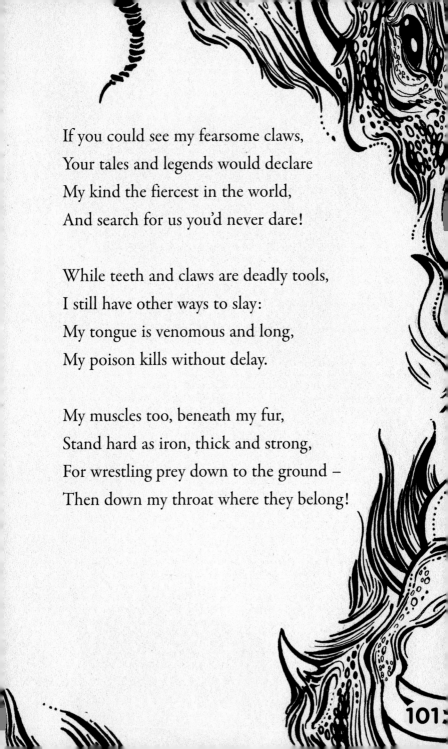

If you could see my fearsome claws,
Your tales and legends would declare
My kind the fiercest in the world,
And search for us you'd never dare!

While teeth and claws are deadly tools,
I still have other ways to slay:
My tongue is venomous and long,
My poison kills without delay.

My muscles too, beneath my fur,
Stand hard as iron, thick and strong,
For wrestling prey down to the ground –
Then down my throat where they belong!

Yes, since the dawn of time my kind
Have hunted, chased and made the kill,
And, underneath the glaring moon,
Have shared the meat and had their fill.

I thought that things would never change,
We'd hunt and eat and sleep, and then
We'd run and play and sleep some more,
Then go and do it all again.

Yet, in the end, our prey grew scarce,
We could not reach fresh feeding sites,
We'd emptied all the land of food,
And starved through long and hungry nights.

One moonless night I stood alone,
My sisters, brothers, all had left,
My limbs were weak, my heartbeat slow,
I fell upon my knees, bereft,

And then a miracle occurred,
My shoulders itched and ached, but why?
The answer came as WINGS burst free,
And bore me up into the sky!

I soared through clouds and past the stars,
So full of joy: alive, ALIVE!
But then I thought, *there are no more*
Like me. For only I'd survived.

My life is lonely, far away,
For none that live can know of me,
Or else they'd hunt me down, to kill
The mighty beast they cannot see.

My life depends on staying lost,
So keep my secret, keep it well,
Or else I'll come to hunt for YOU,
For eaten children cannot tell ...